D0839584

ALSO BY CHEYENNE

Clarity, Wisdom, Harmony: Simple and Concise Tools for Living

Because It Matters: A Guide to Getting Your Life In Order Before You Die

Being in the Moment, audio recording

Evelyn's Way, audio recording

For more information on Cheyenne, visit
www.CheyenneAutumnWhitehorse.com.

TWO DOZEN NEW WAYS

TWO DOZEN NEW WAYS:

*A Simple Guide to Empowering Self
and Embracing Happiness*

CHEYENNE

ISBN: 9798751971724

First printing January 2022

Published by Autumn Productions

Cover design and layout by Elite Authors

—〰—

I dedicate this book to the many people in my life who
have supported me, challenged me,
stretched me, and inspired me.

My J.,
I Celebrate You! o
Love & Light
Cheyenne

There is no better time to begin than now.
—Cheyenne Autumn Whitehorse

1. NO MORE

—∞—

No more

- complaining
- asking, "Who am I?"
- justifying my less-than-graceful attitude
- being someone I am not

2. RESPOND

—᙭—

Respond rather than react. The mind is a powerful tool.

You are in charge of how you use it.

Imagine that someone is filming you during your inter-action. Your way of being goes viral. Everyone gets to see your behavior, hear the tone of your language, and see all your facial expressions and body language.

Here's your chance to make every interaction a good one—one that you can feel good about in the end and happy to have anyone view.

3. LET GO

Make a list of what isn't working in your life.

Take the steps needed to eliminate whatever nonworking things you can as quickly as possible, replacing each one with more of what is working for you in your life.

Examples might be:

- Values someone else imposed
- People who bring you down and are negative
- Behaviors that no longer serve or support you
- Things that are broken or take up space; things that you do not need or enjoy

4. CHOOSE TO

Choose to

- take a breath.
- walk away.
- purge on paper (write it out fast, without proper grammar, and then shred or burn it).
- meditate/pray.

Refuse to let anything or anyone bring out the worst in you. Don't give another person the power to bring out the worst in you. It's just not worth it.

5. RELEASE

Frustration, sadness, fear, anger

Breathe

Cry

Yell

Walk

Run

Sing

Dance

Play

Laugh

Pray

Meditate

6. LOOK FOR THE BEAUTY

Pause and become aware of the simple beauty in

- a flower blooming.
- a bird soaring.
- a sunrise.
- a sunset.
- the glow of the moon.
- the twinkle of the stars in the night sky.

7. BE GRATEFUL

Be grateful...
   for what is working.

8. HONOR

—◊—

Honor
your heart,
your health,
your home,
your relationships,
yourself.

Bring only loving, sweet, warm, delicious words, relationships, and places that radiate goodness into your life.

9. GIVE TIME

—ɯ—

Give time

- to those you respect.
- to those who respect you.
- to things that are important to you.
- to what is worthy of your time.

10. REACH OUT

Make dates with others, be they in person for tea or coffee, a walk at the park, or a conversation on the phone. Discuss and share topics such as:

- Happy memories
- Hobbies
- Sports
- Family
- Relationships
- Health and well-being

11. SHARE THE LOVE

—m—

Think of someone who you feel would enjoy hearing from you. Write them a note; send an email or a text on any random day of the year. It might simply say, *Thinking of you* or *I wanted to pop in and say hello*. Let them know you care about them or perhaps how they have inspired you.

12. LAUGH OUT LOUD

Recall a time that you have laughed until your cheeks hurt. Perhaps share a joke you heard or told once long ago. Watch funny reruns of your favorite cartoons or a YouTube video that makes you laugh right out loud.

13. DANCE

—ɯɯ—

Dance

- in the kitchen.
- in the living room.
- the bedroom.
- outside under the stars.

Put on a song that you love, and just dance!

14. PUT IT TO PAPER

Make a list of what you want to do on a daily, weekly, and monthly basis.

For example:
Stretch
Move
Laugh
Nurture self
Meditate
Hydrate
Eat well
Clear the clutter
Learn
Play
Love
Expand

Place the list where you will see it daily, and let it be a gentle reminder to keep you on track.

15. BE YOUR OWN BEST FRIEND

—ɯ—

Honest
Kind
Loving
Trustworthy
Respectful

Be mindful of your inner voice, and speak with kind words to yourself. Say any—and, if possible, all—of these things to yourself at least once a day. Try taking a long, slow, easy breath in, and as you exhale, speak out loud:

I love you.
I am proud of you.
I respect you.
Thank you for being you.

At the same time, imagine your heart opening, much like the bud of a flower when it receives the sunshine to bloom. Feel it in the center of your being. Smile.

16. GIVE YOURSELF A COMPLIMENT

—⁂—

One that is true.

One that you struggle to receive.

One that you would love to receive from someone you respect.

17. BE REAL

—w—

Embrace what you have with a grateful heart,
and make the best of it.

18. NOURISH YOUR BODY

Sit down.

Be still.

Reflect on the food of which you are about to partake.

Give thanks.

Eat slowly with joyful thoughts.

Savor each and every bite.

19. CREATE MORE

—〰—

Make a list of the things you love:

Colors
Textures
The arts
Hobbies
People
Places

Now do what you can to bring more of them into your life.

20. INSPIRE

Do something to inspire yourself.

Do something to inspire someone else.

Start small.

Do something...anything.

Just begin where you are, and trust the process.

To inspire and to be inspired are awesome feelings.

21. VISION

Big or small…be sure to have one. The sky is the limit! One day at a time, one week at a time, one year at a time, or a lifetime.

See it happening; be your own visionary.

22. YOU'VE GOT THIS

Life does not always go the way you might want it to go. However, you do have the free will to decide how to navigate or manage it. Believe in the power within to regroup, look for support, and discover resources to adapt.

23. CELEBRATE YOURSELF

Learn from regrets and move on to make the most of life in the now. Spend as little time as possible letting the past impose on the future.

24. MAKE IT A GREAT DAY

—ɯ—

Do something for yourself.

Do something for someone else.

Do something you have been putting off.

BONUS

—⚊—

Affirmations

For some people, working with affirmations[1] can be supportive. By repeating and believing in statements, one can make positive changes. Placing a note with a positive or motivational statement on your mirror or the refrigerator door or using one as your screen saver is a time-honored self-help action that can and does work for some people.

However, with that said, it can be frustrating at times to be working with an affirmation such as "Life is good; all is well" if that is not factual for you. Basically, you are telling yourself a lie if that is not what you are experiencing or feeling at the time.

I have worked for years with individuals who have had some very hard times in their lives. Having no one there to listen, support, and provide the love they need can

---

1. An affirmation is the action of process of affirming something or being affirmed; it is emotional support and encouragement.

sometimes create a lack of self-esteem as well as feelings of being unlovable. Some people find themselves feeling resentment, anger, sadness, and ultimately a lack of joy, which may lead to unhealthy self-talk and create issues in relationships with loved ones.

I believe that working with affirmations, using them to give your inner voice a place to be heard, can be supportive, helpful, and healing in the end. It allows the pain to be expressed and validated by the person it matters most to—*yourself.*

No one can validate, honor, and love you in the way you need and desire better than you.

So if you find affirmations to be frustrating and/or not making sense, here is another way of working with them.

Writing Exercise
Write down an affirmation—for example, "Life is good; all is well." Pause for a moment, take a breath in, and then breathe it out. Perhaps say the affirmation out loud—in this case, "Life is good; all is well," repeating it several times.

Ask yourself, "Is this true for me?" If the answer is "No," then notice what you are feeling. Now put pen to paper, or if you are more into using your computer, then start typing your reply to the affirmation. This is your opportunity to speak your truth. An example: If you are not feeling in alignment with the statement "Life is good; all is well," one might reply with something like this: "Life is not so good right now. I am having difficulties at work or at home, or my health is not great."

Write as quickly as possible, with no regard to grammar or sentence structure. Just write it until you have nothing more to say. Rewrite the affirmation. Take a pause and notice whether there is something more you want to express. If so, then repeat the process until you are able to feel at peace with the statement. This might not happen the first time you work with an affirmation in this way. You may do this exercise once a day for a week or once a week for a month; maybe it will take a year. The bottom line is that you are giving your inner voice a chance to be heard.

Why I Decided to Share the Bonus Writing Exercise

Some years back, during my training with the Network of Victim Assistance (NOVA), it just so happened that I was also taking a course on the use of affirmations to heal the inner wounds that one might carry due to past trauma—the idea of writing down an affirmation, re-

peating it daily with a loving voice, that one would believe it, and so it would be. This was a wonderful idea;
however, after completing my NOVA training, I began to
work with victims on the hotline.

Late one night a call came in from a woman who had
been raped. After I got off the call at two o'clock in
the morning, I found myself trying to imagine how one
would integrate the idea of using a positive affirmation,
such as "Life is good; all is well," when someone had such
a horrific experience. How could this help?

Once I was in private practices I began to suggest using
affirmations differently. It was then that I began working
with the writing exercise I just shared with you. Taking
any positive wishful statement that you don't align with
and using it to give your heart and mind a voice can be a
powerful and healing exercise.

Here's hoping this book brings you new ways of thinking, being and loving. I celebrate you.

Love and light,
Cheyenne

Made in the USA
Monee, IL
16 February 2022

90933647R00036